NATURE'S MYSTERIES

TSUNAMIS

DANIEL E. HARMON

Britannica®
Educational Publishing

IN ASSOCIATION WITH

ROSEN
EDUCATIONAL SERVICES

Published in 2019 by Britannica Educational Publishing (a trademark of Encyclopædia Britannica, Inc.) in association with The Rosen Publishing Group, Inc.
29 East 21st Street, New York, NY 10010

Distributed exclusively by Rosen Publishing.
To see additional Britannica Educational Publishing titles, go to rosenpublishing.com.

First Edition

Britannica Educational Publishing
J.E. Luebering: Executive Director, Core Editorial
Mary Rose McCudden: Editor, Britannica Student Encyclopedia

Rosen Publishing
Kathy Kuhtz Campbell: Senior Editor
Michael Moy: Series Designer
Tahara Anderson: Book Layout
Cindy Reiman: Photography Manager
Nicole DiMella: Photo Researcher

Library of Congress Cataloging-in-Publication Data

Names: Harmon, Daniel E., author.
Title: Tsunamis / Daniel E. Harmon.
Description: New York: Britannica Educational Publishing, in Association with Rosen Educational Services, 2019 | Series: Nature's mysteries | Includes bibliographical references and index. | Audience: Grades 1–5.
Identifiers: LCCN 2018016345| ISBN 9781508106654 (library bound) | ISBN 9781508106531 (pbk.) | ISBN 9781508106593 (6 pack)
Subjects: LCSH: Tsunamis—Juvenile literature.
Classification: LCC GC221.5 .H38 2019 | DDC 551.46/37—dc23
LC record available at https://lccn.loc.gov/2018016345

Manufactured in the United States of America

Photo credits: Cover, p. 1 Sadatsugu Tomizawa/AFP/Getty Images; back cover Sylvie Corriveau/Shutterstock.com; p. 4 Mass Communication Specialist 3rd Class Alexander Tidd/U.S. Navy; p. 5 Ernesto Benavides/AFP/Getty Images; p. 6 Doroniuk Anastasiia/Shutterstock.com; p. 7 AFP/Getty Images; p. 8 udaix/Shutterstock.com; pp. 9, 13, 15 The Asahi Shimbun/Getty Images; p. 10 Eduards Normaals/Shutterstock.com; p. 11 mapichai/Shutterstock.com; p. 12 Kyodo News/Getty Images; p. 14 © AP Images; p. 16 USGS; p. 17 Philip A. McDaniel/U.S. Navy; p. 18 Private Collection/Photo © Chris Hellier/Bridgeman Images; p. 19 Hulton Archive/Getty Images; p. 20 Encyclopædia Britannica, Inc.; p. 21 Jack Garofalo/Paris Match Archive/Getty Images; p. 22 Leemage/Universal Images Group/Getty Images; p. 23 Fototeca Storica Nazionale/Hulton Archive/Getty Images; p. 24 askHVO, U.S. Geological Survey; p. 25 EQRoy/Shutterstock.com; p. 26 Noah Seelam/AFP/Getty Images; p. 27 NOAA Teacher at Sea Program; p. 28 Jason Lindesmith/FEMA; p. 29 Designua/Shutterstock.com; interior pages background Maksimilian/Shutterstock.com.

CONTENTS

WAVE OF TERROR

A Pacific island harbor on a sunny day is a water playground. Families swim and frolic in the shallow depths. Surfers paddle out beyond the inlet to find a swelling wave to ride.

Suddenly an alarm shrieks from a pier overlooking the happy scene. Someone with a higher view of the ocean's expanse has noticed an odd formation on the horizon. A solid wall of water appears to have risen above the

On March 11, 2011, a severe earthquake and tsunami destroyed Otsuchi and other areas in northern Japan.

VOCABULARY

In Japanese, the word tsunami means "harbor wave." Tsunamis can cause great destruction when they reach land.

ocean surface. It is as wide as the eye can see. It is racing toward the harbor.

"Tsunami!"

Everyone scrambles from the water. They run through the streets and up the hillside farther inland. They must find high ground, higher than the massive wave can reach.

Already, the ocean surge is crashing through the seaport. It takes down buildings, swirling rubble before it. Can people get to a safe height before it overtakes them, too?

As a tsunami alert sounds, people in Lima, Peru, rush to safety on higher ground by following a marked route.

WHAT ARE TSUNAMIS?

Tsunamis are massive, destructive ocean waves. They begin when a powerful event on the ocean floor pushes tons of water to the surface from below. From that point, they begin to move across the ocean in all directions. They can spread for thousands of miles.

These waves slow down but increase in size and force as they travel. By the time they arrive at a distant seashore,

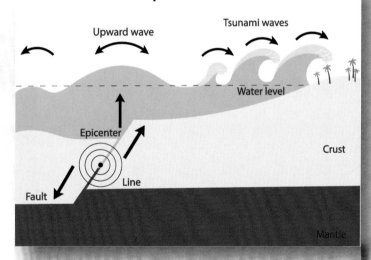

Earthquake Tsunami

Upward wave

Tsunami waves

Water level

Epicenter

Crust

Line

Fault

Mantle

An undersea earthquake forces water from below to the surface and creates waves. The waves get larger and more powerful as they move.

COMPARE AND CONTRAST

Tsunamis sometimes are called tidal waves, but they are not tidal at all. Tides are changes in the ocean levels that are noticeable along the coasts. They are caused by the pull of gravity on Earth's oceans from the moon and sun. The tides occur regularly every day. How are tides similar to tsunamis? How are they different?

A photograph taken from above shows a tsunami's series of waves moving up the Naka River in Japan.

they may be as high as a three-story building.

A tsunami is not just a single wave. It consists of a series of waves following one another. The first wave may not be the strongest. It may be several days until the surface of the ocean returns to normal.

WHAT TRIGGERS A TSUNAMI?

Most tsunamis are caused by earthquakes that occur underwater. These earthquakes result when the sea-floor abruptly shifts at a certain place.

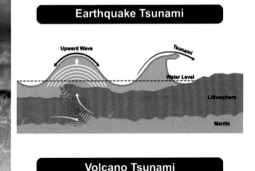

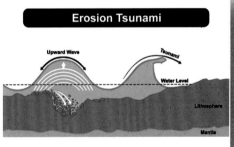

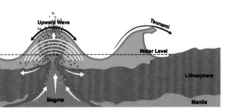

Tsunamis can be triggered by several different types of events. The most common cause is an earthquake.

Tsunamis also can be caused by immense land-slides from high cliffs on a seacoast. Heavy rain over a period of days or weeks can

weaken the soil and bring millions of tons of it crashing into the sea.

Some tsunamis begin as a result of volcanoes. Famous examples throughout history are Mount Tambora in Indonesia in 1815, Mount Krakatoa on Rakata Island between Java and Sumatra in 1883, and Mount Thera in Greece more than 3,500 years ago. Each event caused thousands of deaths.

Nishinoshima, a Japanese volcano, is making a new island in the Pacific Ocean. Some scientists believe that the island could collapse someday and cause a tsunami.

DISRUPTIONS ON THE SEAFLOOR

Tectonic Plates

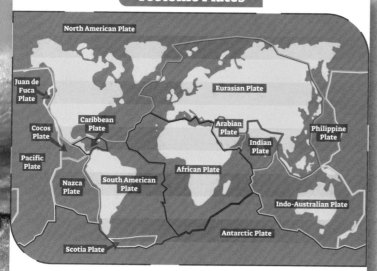

North American Plate
Juan de Fuca Plate
Eurasian Plate
Caribbean Plate
Arabian Plate
Philippine Plate
Cocos Plate
Indian Plate
Pacific Plate
African Plate
Nazca Plate
South American Plate
Indo-Australian Plate
Antarctic Plate
Scotia Plate

Plate Tectonics

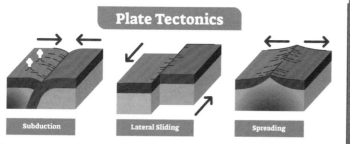

Subduction

Lateral Sliding

Spreading

Earth's outer layer is a system of vast **plates** made of solid rock. The plates slowly, constantly move alongside, over, or away from one another. Sudden shifts near the edges of the plates cause the ground to tremble.

(*Top*) A map shows Earth's tectonic plates. (*Bottom*) The plates can move toward each other, past each other, or away from each other.

Earthquakes release tremendous amounts of energy. If a large earthquake occurs close to the seafloor, it causes great columns of water to rise to the surface. Tsunamis typically are caused by earthquakes that happen not more than 30 miles (50 kilometers) beneath the seafloor.

The power of an earthquake that occurs near the ocean's floor can force enormous amounts of water to the surface.

Underwater Earthquake caused a tsunami

Ground floor uplift

Ground floor collapse

DEADLY WAVES FORM

When an earthquake occurs beneath an ocean, water is forced toward the sea surface. The disturbance that results on the surface begins a system of waves that will spread in a ring pattern across the sea in all directions.

Strong tsunamis can sometimes create whirlpools, which are areas of rapidly swirling water.

THINK ABOUT IT

What else can cause ripples in the surface of a lake or pond?

The event is like the disturbances that occur constantly on ponds, rivers, and other small bodies of water. A fish breaks the surface to catch an insect. From the point of disturbance, a ring of waves forms and spreads outward. The larger the fish, the greater the ripple effect.

There is a tremendous difference between the weight of a fish and the tons of water pushed up by an earthquake. The wave effects caused by a fish jumping begin to diminish within moments. When a tsunami forms and begins to spread, its effects will intensify, or become stronger, sometimes for many hours to come.

It can take days for the ocean to return to normal after a tsunami occurs.

RACING ACROSS THE OCEAN

Tsunami waves roll in toward the Pacific island of Samoa. In some nearby areas, people and cars were swept out to sea.

The power of a tsunami as it moves across the water can be misleading at first. It may be barely noticeable to people aboard ships it passes beneath. That soon changes.

The tsunami builds in strength and **velocity**. Eventually, it can reach speeds up to 500 miles (800 km) an hour. This speed is as fast as some jet airplanes fly. The

tsunami may grow as high as 100 feet (30 meters).

Tsunamis usually slow down as they come near a shoreline. This slowdown happens because the water is shallower there. However, they do not decrease in force.

As the first big wave in the series approaches land, water along the shore may be drawn outward to meet it. Then the wave slams ashore. It sweeps up buildings, trees, automobiles, and everything else in its way.

The force of a tsunami is so powerful that it can move a ship inland and leave it on top of a building.

THE WORST TSUNAMI ON RECORD

On the morning of December 26, 2004, a powerful earthquake shook the seafloor off the coast of Sumatra in the Indian Ocean.

A tsunami formed on the ocean surface above. The first waves were about a foot (30 centimeters) high. But as they began moving across the water, they quickly grew. In less than an

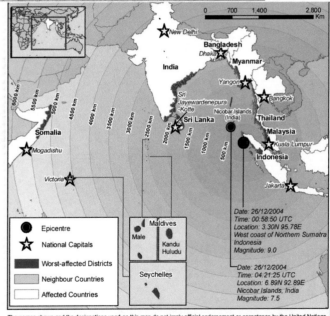

Epicentre

National Capitals

Worst-affected Districts

Neighbour Countries

Affected Countries

Maldives

Male

Kandu Huludu

Seychelles

Date: 26/12/2004
Time: 00:58:50 UTC
Location: 3.30N 95.78E
West coast of Northern Sumatra Indonesia
Magnitude: 9.0

Date: 26/12/2004
Time: 04:21:25 UTC
Location: 6.89N 92.89E
Nicobar Islands, India
Magnitude: 7.5

The names shown and the designations used on this map do not imply official endorsement or acceptance by the United Nations.

The Indian Ocean tsunami of 2004 traveled from the coast of Indonesia to East Africa.

THINK ABOUT IT

Why do you think so many people died in the tsunami of 2004? How many people do you think live in the area?

hour, the lead wave reached the Sumatra coast. It was nearly 30 feet (9 m) high.

By the time people playing on beaches heard the fierce roar of the coming wall of water, they had only moments to flee. At the port of Banda Aceh, the tsunami swept 1.2 miles (2 km) inland. The city was totally destroyed.

The waves eventually reached more than a dozen countries. The tsunami killed at least 225,000 people and destroyed farms, villages, and resorts throughout the area.

The 2004 tsunami devastated much of the western coast of the Aceh province in Indonesia.

OTHER DEADLY INDIAN OCEAN TSUNAMIS

People who live in coastal cities and villages along the rim of the Indian Ocean well know the danger of tsunamis. So did their ancestors centuries before them.

Another historic tsunami devastated Sumatra on February 10, 1797. Many houses were destroyed. People climbed trees to get above the water. Some died of exposure in the branches.

One surprising result of the disaster occurred on the Batang

This 1881 drawing of a tsunami shows the power of waves, which can easily toss people, boats, and big ships.

Arau River, near Padang in western Sumatra. One large wave carried a massive English ship from its anchorage, up the river to a distance of approximately two-thirds of a mile (1 km).

The eruption of the Krakatoa volcano on August 26–27, 1883, is believed to have created the loudest noise in modern history. It was heard 3,000 miles (4,800 km) away. The explosion triggered a series of tsunamis. The greatest wave reached a height of 120 feet (37 m) and killed some 36,000 people.

The 1883 eruption of Krakatoa set in motion a series of tsunamis that hit as far away as Hawaii.

TSUNAMIS IN THE PACIFIC

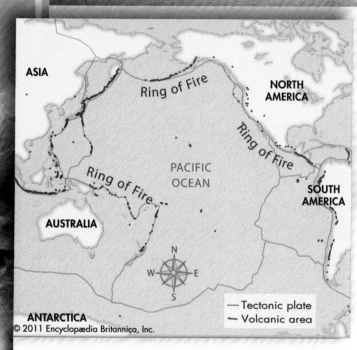

The Ring of Fire is the chain of volcanoes in the Pacific Ocean that erupt in fiery explosions. This area also has earthquakes that can trigger tsunamis.

A chain of volcanoes, known as the Ring of Fire, surrounds the Pacific Ocean. The earthquakes and volcanic activity that are typical in this region can result in devastating tsunamis.

In September 1498 an earthquake sent tsunami surges along the Japanese coast. At least thirty-one thousand people were killed.

More than forty thousand people died on the island of Taiwan in the 1782 South China

COMPARE AND CONTRAST

Most tsunamis occur in the Pacific Ocean. Why do you think it has more tsunamis than other oceans?

Sea tsunami. One record from the time claims sea water destroyed three cities and twenty villages.

An immense earthquake shook the seafloor off the Chilean coast on May 22, 1960. It was the most powerful earthquake in history, according to the US Geological Survey. Within fifteen minutes, 80-foot (25-m) waves smashed the shore. About 1,600 people died as a result of the earthquake and tsunami.

The Chile earthquake of 1960 created a tsunami that killed many Chileans. It also sent tsunamis to Hawaii and Japan.

In 1964 a 9.2 magnitude earthquake struck south-central Alaska. The massive quake set off tsunamis that caused damage as far away as Crescent City, California.

TSUNAMIS IN OTHER REGIONS

La Catastrophe de Nesdal (Norvège)
UNE FALAISE QUI S'ÉCROULE. — NOMBREUSES VICTIMES

In 1905 a mountain rockslide in a fjord caused a tsunami that killed more than sixty people in southern Norway.

Although most tsunamis take place in the Pacific and Indian oceans, tsunamis can ravage any ocean in the world. The Atlantic Ocean has produced a number of memorable tsunamis.

Some eight thousand years ago, a colossal underwater landslide occurred off the coast of Norway. It produced a tsunami that affected islands and coastal areas between Norway and Scotland. In Norway's fjords, surrounded by craggy heights, rockslides have been known to cause smaller tsunamis.

A series of earthquakes occurred in Lisbon, Portugal, on November 1, 1755.

The earthquakes generated waves that traveled west to Martinique in the Caribbean Sea and east to Algiers in northern Africa. The disasters resulted in about sixty thousand dead in Lisbon alone.

In December 1908, an earthquake shook the seafloor of the Strait of Messina, the waterway between Italy and Sicily. The quake triggered an underwater landslide. The landslide caused a tsunami with waves as tall as 40 feet (13 m). The disasters almost completely destroyed the area around the strait. The death toll from the earthquake and tsunami was more than eighty thousand.

In 1908 a strong earthquake was followed by a tsunami that crashed down on the coasts of Sicily and southern Italy.

THE FIRST TSUNAMI WARNING EFFORTS

Thomas Jaggar was the founder of a volcano **observatory** in Hawaii. In 1923, he warned the harbormaster at Hilo that an earthquake had occurred on the east coast of Kamchatka in Russia. Jaggar believed this event could send a destructive ocean wave that would impact the Hawaiian Islands.

Thomas Jaggar founded the Hawaiian Volcano Observatory. The construction of the observatory began in 1912.

His warning was ignored, and at least one Hawaiian fisherman died. Jaggar's effort was the first known attempt to warn of a coming tsunami. But ocean scientists, especially in the Pacific, began to consider warning systems. Japanese researchers issued what may have been the first precautionary advice: "If the ground shakes violently, evacuate." In 1933 the advice was put to the test. An earthquake shook the ground, and many coastal residents evacuated to high ground. Many lives were saved.

Installing tsunami warning systems like this siren system in Hawaii has saved countless lives.

MODERN WARNING SYSTEMS

Today many countries, including the United States, have tsunami warning systems. In 1949 the Pacific Tsunami Warning Center was established in Hawaii. At first it was just used by the United States. Since 1965, however, it has served as the warning center for 26 countries.

India's Tsunami Early Warning Centre uses the newest systems to sound timely warnings of earthquakes and tsunamis.

Following the disaster of December 2004, government organizations set a goal of establishing similar systems for the Indian Ocean and eventually the entire globe.

The warning systems rely on monitors that detect movements in the earth. The monitors can measure where earthquakes

This buoy is part of a tsunami warning system. It receives signals from a monitor on the ocean floor and sends them to a satellite that relays them to stations on land.

take place and how strong they are. If an earthquake above a certain strength occurs near a coast, a tsunami warning immediately is issued. Scientific instruments can determine whether a tsunami actually forms. If not, or if it is weak, the warning is canceled.

FLEE THE DANGER

There is no way to stop a tsunami. However, people can take actions to protect themselves from the dangers of tsunamis. People who live in at-risk coastal areas are urged to pay attention to tsunami warnings. They should head for high ground if possible. Anyone who is at the beach or near the ocean and feels the Earth shake should immediately move to higher ground, rather than wait for a warning to be issued.

Sometimes before a tsunami strikes, the water near the shore

Evacuation route signs can help guide people on a safe route to higher ground or a shelter to escape a tsunami.

THINK ABOUT IT

If a tsunami happens in a low coastal area where there is no high ground to go to for safety, where else could you go where it is high?

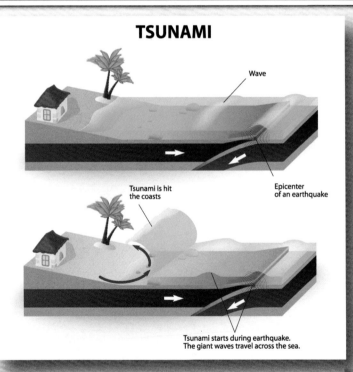

TSUNAMI

Wave

Epicenter of an earthquake

Tsunami is hit the coasts

Tsunami starts during earthquake. The giant waves travel across the sea.

Before an approaching tsunami, water is pulled away from the shore. The wave's peak will hit the shore very soon after that.

is pulled out to sea and the seafloor is exposed. This may attract curious people and fishers to the seafloor. People should never stay near the shore to explore during such periods. The crest, or peak, of the wave will arrive very quickly, leaving no time to escape.

GLOSSARY

ANCHORAGE A place where a ship is held secure by its anchor.

COLOSSAL Of very great size; gigantic.

CRAGGY Noted for steep, rugged rocks or cliffs.

DEVASTATE To destroy much or most of something.

DISRUPTION A problem that throws something into disorder.

DISTANT Far away.

EXPOSURE The condition of leaving without shelter, protection, or care.

HARBORMASTER An official appointed to supervise activities in a harbor.

IMMENSE Very great in size or amount.

LANDSLIDE A large amount of earth, rock, and other material that moves down a steep slope.

MAGNITUDE The size or extent of something.

MONITOR A device that constantly measures movements.

PRECAUTIONARY Caution taken in advance.

RAVAGE To attack or act upon with great violence

SURGE A swelling, rolling, or sweeping forward.

FOR MORE INFORMATION

Books

Furgang, Kathy. *Everything Volcanoes and Earthquakes* (National Geographic Kids). Washington, DC: National Geographic Children's Books, 2013.

McAneney, Caitie. *Slammed by Tsunamis* (Natural Disasters: How People Survive). New York, NY: PowerKids Press, 2018.

Spilsbury, Louise, and Richard Spilsbury. *Tsunami Crushes Coastline* (Earth Under Attack!). New York, NY: Gareth Stevens Publishing, 2018.

Squire, Ann. *Tsunamis* (True Book). New York, NY: Children's Press, 2016.

Woolf, Alex. *The Science of Natural Disasters: The Devastating Truth About Volcanoes, Earthquakes, and Tsunamis.* New York, NY: Franklin Watts, 2018.

Websites

Do Something.org

"11 Facts About Tsunamis"

https://www.dosomething.org/us/facts/11-facts-about-tsunamis

National Geographic Kids

"Tsunami Facts: Check Out the Mighty Wave!"

https://www.natgeokids.com/au/discover/geography/physical-geography/tsunamis/#!/register

Weather Wiz Kids

"Tsunami Questions"

http://www.weatherwizkids.com/?page_id=100

INDEX